A Play

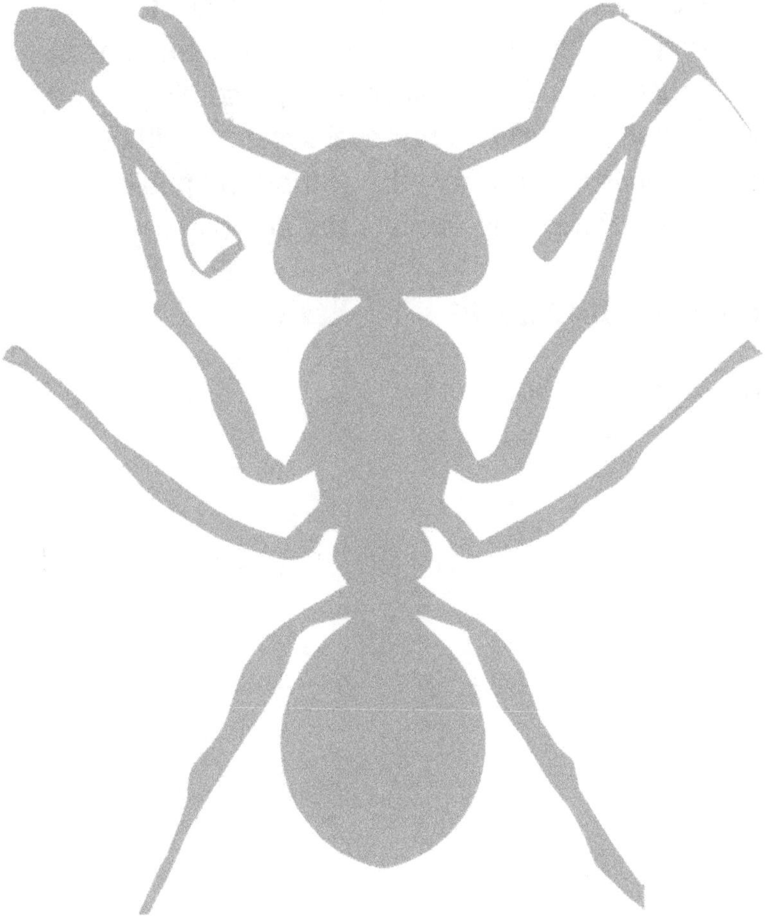

Conversation

ISI AGBOAYE

ISBN: 978-1-906963-33-0

For copies of this play, contact the author

Phone: +447817629683

Printed in Great Britain

Contents

The Context

As a child, I was fascinated by conversations in my part of Africa. Such conversations happened everywhere. They were dramatic and interesting. I have grown to appreciate the meanings embedded in such conversations which in traditional understanding are bountifully echoed in Esan folktale performance sessions. In other words, whatever you are told in real conversations in Esan would likely be resonated in fun-filled formal or informal storytelling events in the community.

It is interesting to note that the meanings embedded in such conversations consciously or unconsciously steered the collectives towards order, or some sort of change and development within the traditional context. The conversations were dramatic, touching on issues that reminded us about ourselves. It is such tradition that I am following in my creative interpretations; thus, acknowledging the anecdotal stance that, every conversation is a performance and every performance is a conversation in my part of Africa.

So, if you are ready, let us dig into issues that metaphorically mirror the state of our nation, illuminate our conversation, and move us closer to finding tangible meanings that would possibly direct our minds towards real independence and tangible development. I dare to postulate in this creative effort that there is hope for the whole of Africa, if we are willing to learn from the ants, our silent and hardworking neighbours.

The Plot

A group of ants are mandated by the Creator of all things to sanitise and reform the collectives of a failing nation; thereby putting them consciously on the unambiguous path of genuine Independence and development. Ancestor, a mythical character is sent from an unidentified intelligent part of the Universe to coordinate the process. He is assisted by Acolyte, one of the corrupt elements in the nation as the ants work mostly behind the scenes to teach the inhabitants of the nation how to achieve real change and development. Meanwhile, the whole nation is evacuated, and the people are quarantined underground in camps set up by ants for necessary sanitization as the development process instigate conversations in different forms.

Dedication

For Dr Victor Ukaegbu

Thanks for being a kind academic guide

You may be gone, but not forgotten.

The Characters

- Ancestor - the one who has come to co-ordinate change in an imagined dysfunctional nation
- The Creator - akin to God, the Creator of all things
- Ants in Chorus
- Acolyte - Ancestor's assistant
- The Questioner
- The Helpful one
- The Wailing one

(The Questioner, The Helpful one and The Wailing one are all human reflectors who mirror events in the nation)

- The Evil bird - may be seen or unseen
- The Shadows - a group of three to six performers or more who enact improvised roles within the context and spirit of Community Theatre

PART 1

The beginning of the Narrative

(A minimalist setting, suggesting a rural or semi-urban setting with few rusty roofs and thatched houses in a distance).

Ants in Chorus:

We have got some work to do
We will help to sort things out
We are ready
Ever ready
To sort things out for all
We will fix the young and old
Women - yes
Men - yes
Even children too

We have got the mandate
We will do things well

We have got the mandate
We will do things well
We have got the mandate
We will do things well
We are moving here
We are moving there
We are moving everywhere

(Chorus is repeated twice as the ants parade around the stage and exit).

The Wailing one:

What an impressive parade. Should I say, 'Once upon a time' or should I say, 'It happened suddenly?' It happened suddenly after a long period of frustration and deprivation.

The Helpful one:

Who is listening, who is listening and learning?

The Wailing one:

Somebody said, 'If you throw a stone in the marketplace, it will hit a graduate.' That goes to show that some of our people are well educated and extremely talented, but why are they languishing in the periphery? Those who should be leading are being badly led, and many who occupy the centre hardly know how to make or share the national resources. So, the centre seems static. Not much is being delivered to hungry children and poverty is written on so many faces. Why? Some can't take it; they are taking their own lives meaninglessly.

The Helpful one:

Who is listening, who is listening and learning?

The Wailing one:

There is so much wealth in the centre, but little or nothing for others. It never used to be like that. Where did all the wealth go? I know that we sold loads of crude oil in the seasons of boom; now, it seems we are doomed. So, who are those specifically steering the ship of this nation? Pity, they can hardly hold firmly to the faltering ship.

The Helpful one:

Who is listening, who is listening and learning?

The Questioner:

What should the people have done to liberate the nation?

(The shadows appear on stage and enact imagined acts of what the people should have done to liberate the nation).

Why did you carefully edit the story of the oldest woman in the nation? Your outline is not fair to the old woman. Your outline left out important details, important details. You did not add that we should have listened to her predictions, proclaiming that the whole nation would be swept away by forces that are greater than the might of those wielding massive guns that blow out the ear drums and keep many flattened on the ground - dead. She predicted that the politicians would be punished for treating the nation badly. Unfortunately, she died of starvation, and many people remember her as the evil witch. An evil witch, speaking the truth? She was thrown into the steady flow of the River Niger; a woman who should have been buried decently. The old woman did not understand what democracy means; but she suggested that the government of the people should fend for the people.

The Wailing one:

At least they showed that we do not understand what Democracy means; a necessary tool for change and development. They also added that we do not know how to vote, count the votes or the skills to watch closely when votes are being counted. They showed that votes are always terribly rigged, and those who should be steering the ship towards the right course are pushed aside while those who have little or no experience are positioned in front of the wheel. I am making notes. That is why we have crashed on this massive boulder, having gone in circles for too long.

The Helpful one:

Who is listening, who is listening and learning?

The Questioner:

What should the people have done to liberate the nation?

(The shadows appear on stage and enact imagined acts of what the people should have done to liberate themselves).

The Wailing one:

I am happy you showed that there is hardly clean water to drink and functional electricity. There are extremely rich folks who boast of massive mansions, expensive cars, fantastic jets; still, there are countless poor folks living in the same towns and cities who stretch out their battered plates, begging for a day's meal.

The Questioner:

What should the people have done to liberate the nation?

(The shadows appear on stage and enact imagined acts of what the people should have done to liberate themselves).

The Wailing one:

Thanks for giving a splendid representation of the schoolteachers. They are hardly paid for months. Other civil servants die, waiting for their meagre salaries or pension. You saw them walking about like folks with severe stomachache. Yes, stomachache from hunger and extreme poverty in a nation that should be flowing with milk and honey. In all these, you saw programmed party folks with placards and feigned faces in perpetual celebration, creating the impression that all is well.

The Helpful one:

Who is listening, who is listening and learning?

The Questioner:

What should the people have done to liberate the nation?

(The shadows appear on stage and enact imagined notions of what the people should have done to liberate themselves).

The Wailing one:

Did you see that some schools are battered and leaking? The hospitals have little or nothing to offer after so many years of Independence. Those who hoard all the money have specific rooms reserved in luxurious hospitals in western nations, but there are hardly pillows in the hospital wards and basic medication for ordinary people in the nation. You've seen how we are wrapped in the cloak of dependence; even the smallest things are imported from western nations.

Ants in Chorus:

We have got some work to do
We will help to sort things out
We are ready
Ever ready

To sort things out for all
We will fix the young and old
Women - yes
Men - yes
Even children too

We have got the mandate
We will do things well
We have got the mandate
We will do things well
We have got the mandate
We will do things well
We are moving here
We are moving there
We are moving everywhere

(Chorus is repeated twice as the ants parade around the stage and exit).

The Helpful one:
Who is listening, who is listening and learning?

The Questioner:
What should the people have done to liberate the nation?

(The shadows appear on stage and enact imagined acts of what the people should have done to liberate themselves).

The Wailing one:

Did you see images of extreme religiosity? Don't imagine that everything would be perfect because we call on God every minute. The norm is to pretend that you are religious even when you cheat others and commit heinous crimes against the community, like robbery, kidnapping, ritual murder - all orchestrated by uncharted indoctrination and superstitious beliefs.

The Helpful one:

Who is listening, who is listening and learning?

The Questioner:

What should the people have done to liberate the nation?

(The shadows appear on stage and enact imagined notions of what the people should have done to liberate themselves).

The Wailing one:

You saw revealing scenes. Not everything works here. Many people - especially the young ones aspire to travel by any means necessary out of the country - particularly through the Sahara Desert to find solace in western nations. As we speak, many may be trying to cross the fierce Sahara Desert, and many may be dying in the Mediterranean ocean trying to cross the sea in makeshift boats. Some of those who survived the blazing heat and dragging dust of the Sahara Desert are busy selling sex in

Europe to those who should not be ravaging their nakedness and denigrating their pride in the first place.

The Helpful one:

Who is listening, who is listening and learning?

The Questioner:

What should the people have done even in such circumstances?

(The shadows appear on stage and enact imagined acts of what the people should have done in such circumstances).

Ants in Chorus:

We have got some work to do
We will help to sort things out
We are heading to the East
We are heading West
We are heading to the South and North
We are fixing one and all

We have got the mandate
We will do things well
We have got the mandate
We will do things well
We have got the mandate
We will do things well

We are moving here
We are moving there
We are moving everywhere

(Chorus is repeated twice as the ants parade around the stage and exit).

The Wailing one:

Your enactment is right. We have tested all forms of governance - civilian and military. What about the frustrating impact of bribery, corruption, and bad governance? We are trapped, seriously trapped.

The Questioner:

What should the people have done to liberate the nation?

(The shadows appear on stage and enact imagined acts of what the people should have done to liberate themselves).

The Wailing one:

Dysfunction. That's the best word you should have inscribed on your placards. Dysfunction. In a drinking house down the road, someone suggested that a lockdown would sort things out for the nation. He added that everybody should be temporarily sent to a neighbouring country so the nation would be restructured. All the drinkers laughed and laughed for many minutes till they started vomiting all they had eaten and drunk.

The Helpful one:

Who is listening, who is listening and learning?

The Wailing one:

They are coming to rule us again.

The Helpful one:

(Wipes his face with the back of his left hand as if trying to see clearly). Who?

The Wailing one:

Ohhh - they are coming again - ships and ships stretching as far as the eye can see.

The Questioner:

What should we do with those who changed our tongues forever and drove us from the centre, leaving us confused in the periphery?

(The shadows appear on stage and enact imagined acts of what the people should have done to liberate themselves).

You should have added that the old woman prophesied that they would be back. She said that our nation is such a beautiful place with lovely fields and organic foods. She predicted that their children and grandchildren are coming to stay and help us build our nation. Her narrative was like detestable bile to our minds. Why should their children and grandchildren come back to taunt us afresh many asked? She predicted that they would be kind this time; they would be good for the nation. She spoke about wildfires and floods raging in the nations of the visitors who are coming to stay in our land. She told us that she saw massive stones being hurled in the air and trees flung as far as the eyes could see. We did not believe a word. She added that only a few who run into waiting ships would survive. Her quivering voice kept echoing for days, saying that they are coming - that they are coming for good, having escaped the terror of nature in nations that were once beautiful and lovely.

The Helpful one:

Are you suggesting that they should be allowed into our nation? They should not be allowed in. We will restructure the nation and know how to manage ourselves, and how to negotiate sensibly.

The Wailing one:

True.

The Questioner:

Did you speak to any of them?

The Wailing one:

They are waiting off the coast in thousands.

The Questioner:

Did you read their minds?

The Wailing one:

They said they have not come to conquer; that they have only come to seek refuge. They said nations of the earth are shrinking in size. They spoke about terrible volcanoes and massive surge of boiling water destroying their part of the earth.

The Questioner:

That's unfortunate. Let's concentrate on our domestic affairs. But how and why did our forebears go wrong?

(The shadows appear on stage and enact imagined notions of how our forebears negotiated badly with the colonialists).

The Wailing one:

Hmmm. We trusted them in the past - but they changed swiftly like the chameleon. They came conquering and looting and snatching all we knew from our hearts and minds. How fortunate; it appears that we are the only ones left in the universe; the only safe place on earth.

The Helpful one:

It might be useful to speak to them. They are very many; men, women, and children - all eager to troop into the nation.

The Wailing one:

Troop into the nation - just like that? Meanwhile, they cannot come into this state of dysfunction.

The Helpful one:

Who knows, they may be useful to us. That stimulates my thinking.

The Wailing one:

Think about it - nothing has worked in the centre since they abandoned us in the periphery. Unfortunately, those who had the solution where looked upon as the real troublemakers and the land continued to degenerate uncontrollably. The nation became a place for neo-colonialist agents who took advantage of the weak centre to dictate how the nation should be despicably milked. The people groaned and suffered. That is why many young people were forced to travel across the Sahara Desert to be enslaved in nations whose forebears dragged our brothers and sisters across the Atlantic Ocean - ripping them of their identities in the guise of introducing civilization, and thoroughly schooling them to hate everything that defined them. Where they protested, the power of the whip and guns spoke and silenced them forever. After many years, they were all ceremoniously wrapped into a commonwealth where the wealth was not common. I am tired of waving flags sown by tailors that do not have our interest at heart. I want to be appreciated as somebody, to have a stake in the things that make us grow and glow.

The Helpful one:

It's disheartening. You would have thought things would change when the colonisers left.

The Wailing one:

Sad - sad indeed.

The Helpful one:

We also colonised ourselves with the script the colonisers left in the minds of the ruling class.

The Wailing one:

Obvious complication.

The Helpful one:

Perhaps the politicians were ill-prepared or were not capable of reading the map of nationhood.

The Wailing one:

Why should you starve your children and offer nothing to your workers? How would you frustrate the aged and promise the nation nothing but pain, fear and hunger? We could not even handle little projects - bridges, dams, railroads the colonialists left for us. The long campaign speeches of the politicians did not save us; yet there were rolls upon rolls of speeches that did not matter much. Bridges crumbled, roads were battered, stomachs are empty, and fields not cultivated. Our engineers were not prepared or schooled to produce bolts and our agriculturists do not know how to farm peanuts.

The Questioner:

What should the people have done to liberate the nation?

(The shadows appear on stage and enact imagined notions of what the people should have done to liberate themselves).

The Helpful one:

Daily, we wallowed in the quicksand of disaffection, frustration, confusion, and distractions. As if that's not enough, we welcomed one leader after another - one liar after another and nothing seemed to work. Our politicians kept running back to the ones whose scripts promised us everything, devalued our money and put us in serious debt. So, who will pay back the billions borrowed by the politicians?

The Wailing one:

Oh God, the politicians squandered, plundered and battered the nation.

The Helpful one:

We could not do anything because their security operatives pointed guns at us.

The Wailing one:

Why should they points guns at us for asking why billions of pounds and dollars were stashed in foreign banks while many suffered in the nation? We should have asked why our politicians kept asking for loans when a few of them could provide all the money the nation needed.

The Helpful one:

Yes. You're right.

The Wailing one:

They stole, they squandered - they stole, they squandered - they stole, they squandered.

The Helpful one:

They hid some in the accounts of friends and families everywhere, and buried some in graves, borrow-pits, and abandoned houses. When a group of people tried to stop this tortoise syndrome, they were branded enemies of the people. This is the sad scenario we found ourselves. If you have ever met the trickster, that is exactly whom our politicians are. The trickster keeps oppressing the people and creating the impression that he can get away with any crime. He gave them a little, kept the rest; gave them a little, kept the rest till he died, and his sons and relatives took over from him. They gave us a little, kept the rest; they gave us a little, kept the rest; they gave us a little, kept the rest; they gave us a little, kept the rest - till they finally took everything - the people still made songs, danced and celebrated Democracy. The trickster regime bloated sick.

The Wailing one:

The trickster regime bloated sick.

Ants in Chorus:

We have got some work to do
We will help to sort things out
We are heading to the East
We are heading West
We are heading to the South and North
We are fixing one and all

(Chorus is repeated twice as the ants parade around the stage and exit).

We have got the mandate
We will do things well

We have got the mandate
We will do things well
We have got the mandate
We will do things well
We are moving here
We are moving there
We are moving everywhere

(Chorus is repeated twice as the ants parade around the stage and exit).

PART 2

The Creator Intervenes

(A massive rumble of thunder and flashing of lightning spread through the stage).

The Creator:

Listen. I heard your rantings about your embittered dispositions and have decided to do something. Enough is enough. I am sending Ancestor from a distant part of the universe. He will coordinate the new dawn, working with Acolyte, a face that you are all familiar with. I have empowered the ants - your neighbours to teach you their ways. They are humble, hardworking, happy, organised, thoughtful, coordinated, creative, independent, helpful, not superstitious, reliable, and always building intelligently.

(Acolyte and Ancestor appear. The sound of a dirge echoes from afar).

Acolyte:

Don't weep in my ears. I tried my best for all of you. By the way, what part am I supposed to play in all these?

Ancestor:

You are my assistant.

Acolyte:

Is this another coup or the shadow of another military regime?

Ants in Chorus:

We have got some work to do
We will help to sort things out
We are heading to the East
We are heading West
We are heading to the South and North
We are fixing one and all

We have got the mandate
We will do things well
We have got the mandate
We will do things well
We have got the mandate
We will do things well
We are moving here
We are moving there

We are moving everywhere

(Chorus is repeated twice as the ants parade around the stage and exit).

Ancestor:

This is a different programme. The tears of the people turned into a steady stream, and their complaints and dirges echoed ceaselessly in the presence of the Creator for so many years.

Acolyte:

We experienced a lot in the past. We saw coups upon Coups; yet nothing changed. Even when we switched to democracy, things became worse. Prayers are not easily answered in this part of the world; many have prayed and prayed and died praying. Their prayers were not answered.

Ancestor:

Things will be different now. The Creator of the universe sent me to help clean out the dirty stable for good.

Acolyte:

What sort of technology are you operating on?

Ancestor:

The power of nature, my friend - the dynamic power of nature.

Acolyte:

I might start taking you seriously if I see something different. This is exactly what the soldiers could not do. Different regimes were tainted with corruption. It took the Creator to intervene; what a great project.

Ants in Chorus:

We have got some work to do
We will help to sort things out
We are heading to the East
We are heading West
We are heading to the South and North
We are fixing one and all

We have got the mandate
We will do things well
We have got the mandate
We will do things well
We have got the mandate
We will do things well
We are moving here
We are moving there
We are moving everywhere

(Chorus is repeated twice as the ants parade around the stage and exit).

The Helpful one:

This is a new regime. The nation has come to a standstill; both the young and old are crawling into ant holes. They are taking instructions from the ants. As we speak, the nation is being abandoned and locked down.

Acolyte:

I believe. We all asked for help, but we were denied. Our oppressors have always been too powerful for us. They had all the guns and the weapons supplied by nations who in turn used them against us.

The Helpful one:

The ants are so organised; the nation is being abandoned.

Acolyte:

What is happening? Where are they going?

Ancestor:

I will explain. It's supernatural - it's swift and it's effective. Gradually, the whole nation is being fumigated and evacuated. They are now filing into several ant holes to pass through the necessary process in camps set up underground by ants. It's tedious, but it's possible. Who could have been able to do this? It's going to be successful.

(Acolyte kneels and greets Ancestor).

That will not be necessary. We have a lot of work to do; and the time frame for this task is one week.

Acolyte:

One week? We have been independent for more than fifty years and still not developed.

Ancestor:

You mean this nation has been independent for many years?

Acolyte:

Exactly.

Ancestor:

I am the Creator's special servant. The Creator deposited everything in me, and I am prepared to work, based on the collective will of the people.

Acolyte

I must be getting a share of these special powers.

Ancestor:

You were specially prepared for this task.

Acolyte:

Does the Creator know me?

Ancestor:

Yes. The Creator sees your thoughts - they are displayed in front of a special screen. It's not that your hands are clean; but there is a purpose for everything. When the Creator of the whole universe looked at this direction, you were picked to prove a point.

Acolyte:

I remain loyal; I feel honoured. The Creator of the whole world knows me (Laughs). I must be special in certain ways. Heeee. The evil bird is passing.

Ancestor:

Stay focused. Play your part and do not hesitate to follow all instructions. Close your eyes - open your eyes - close your eyes, open your eyes.

(Suddenly, the corrupt politicians appear, and Acolyte is frightened).

(They freeze)

The Helpful one:

The politicians and corrupt business folks are being dragged to jail by the ants.

Acolyte:

How did you do that?

Ancestor:

Special disposition and innate genius.

Acolyte:

The ants are awesome. Imagine what puny little ants can do in a massive nation.

Ancestor:

They can do great things. Everlasting jail; that's where they belong forever.

Acolyte:

Forever? Why are they not being asked to file into ant holes like others?

Ancestor:

They have completed their work on earth woefully and failed the Creator who gave them the opportunity to help others.

The Helpful one:

They deserve the punishment; take a good look Acolyte and see what they are going through.

(They freeze as the Shadows enact how the politicians were being treated by the ants).

Acolyte:

Done. Screaming and weeping like children. Grinding their teeth as if they are in hell. You should see their mouth foaming and oozing of foul odour. Hmmm the Creator is powerful. See their mouths forming different shapes, their nostrils dripping, and blood oozing from their ears. It's like they have been there for several years, defecating on themselves. Haaaa - how did you do that? At this point in time, they would have been seated in their limousines, official cars or private jets criss-crossing the whole earth doing nothing for the people. Now, they are trapped by powers beyond their imagination. There is power - there is power and there is power. I have an opinion, but I would rather remain silent. Obviously, they are reaping what they sowed.

Ancestor:

Watch closely, see what's going on.

(The shadows appear on stage and enact imagined acts reflecting the activities of the ants).

Acolyte:

Whatever you are doing is working wonders. The people are willingly filing into ant holes and the ants are welcoming them. The ants are setting up institutions for them. They are being given books - but the books look different; obviously leaves and barks from trees. I never knew you could read leaves and barks from trees. Strange indeed. When did ants have such great knowledge?

Ancestor:

Do not underestimate the power of the Creator of all things. Those were manuscripts we wrote many years ago. You all abandoned them - but the ants preserved them. Even when fragments of them were destroyed by the colonizers in all parts of Africa, some were preserved by the ants in their kingdoms. Do not for once think that others must speak for the Creator who sees and hears everything. The Creator can speak and make things happen.

Acolyte:

I am simply amazed. I am utterly surprised and re-schooled.

Ancestor:

Fumigate the whole nation and run around the whole length and breadth of the nation. Make sure none is left in the nation.

(Acolyte runs in and out of the stage as he chants).

Acolyte:

It must be done - it must be done. My eyes have seen great wonders and I must obey. It must be done - it must be done. My eyes have seen great wonders and I must obey. It must be done - it must be done. My eyes have seen great wonders and I must obey. Done. Heeee - the evil bird.

Ancestor:

Here, drink this and renew your strength.

Acolyte:

Thanks. I have never had any drink as refreshing as this. It's always been all sorts of sophisticated gins imported from other nations. We have always been drinking and getting drunk and doing things their own way.

Ancestor:

This is the time to bring in the surveyors and the town planners. (He speaks into a cow horn as if communicating with someone). Go bring them in - they are waiting. They have completed their training and sanitization.

(Acolyte walks out and comes in piloting the shadows who guide some imaginary folks onto the stage and out again; presumably into the new nation).

Acolyte:

What else?

Ancestor:

They have now been empowered to play their part in preparation for the builders.

Acolyte:

You think they will not ask for bribes anymore? I know a few of them there who would not undertake any project without asking for bribes.

Ancestor:

No. That era is gone for good. The ants were empowered thousands of years ago to impart the ability to hate bribes. They have taken adequate lessons.

Acolyte:

Look at them; look at them going into action; just like the ants. There seems to be renewed vigour to operate in a new way. This is interesting. We have never seen this before. There has never been such dedication and aptitude to work.

Ancestor:

The best is yet to come. In the next few years, the whole nation would be transformed. One will play their part and others will follow. The collective will must prevail to turn the nation in the best direction. They lost it; they are getting it back. The engineers are ready. Bring them in. Let them begin to generate power; let the electric generators begin to roll. Let them be linked with appropriate timing fused to the power of the sun. Water must now begin to flow to all and sundry and the land must be thoroughly irrigated. There must be clean water for all, and the waterways must be kept functional throughout the year.

Acolyte:

Awesome. The nation is moving on the right track. I am happy that you are here. I am happy that you are here for good. Heeee. The evil bird.

Ancestor:

Stay focused.

Acolyte:

Yes. I am focused.

Ancestor:

I am happy that the first group of women have moved from the ant holes to the new nation. It's time to bring the other women into the new nation.

Acolyte:

Is it really time to bring the other women in? What could they have learnt in a short space of time? Do you really know them?

Ancestor:

Bring them in. They are primed to be great learners who will do great things. Unfortunately, they were never given the opportunity to display their knowledge. What could they achieve in an environment that is corrupt to the core?

Acolyte:

You do not know those women. One of them stole the nation deaf and blind. She was sitting in her mansion of gold drinking Krosekko, eating fried chicken and crying crocodile tears.

Ancestor:

Bring them in. They have been programmed to use their great strength to steer the nation towards survival. There is hardly any task they cannot do. They have been better programmed by the ants to do even more. They will fly rockets and go beyond the moon. They will help with the latest machines useful for maximizing efforts. They are great champions.

Acolyte:

I am still not convinced. (Shouts out to the ants). Bring the other women into the new nation.

(The shadows guide a group of unseen people from a point designated as the entrance to the ant holes and camps set up by the ants to an exit designated as the entrance to the new nation).

Ancestor:

You better be convinced. It's a new dispensation. It's time to bring in the youths.

Acolyte:

The youths?

Ancestor:

Yes, the youths.

Acolyte:

They are as lazy as...

Ancestor:

Not this breed of youths. They have not been lazy. They had the ability to undertake all vices with their old and rusty computers. They were known all over the world for their crooked business deals and scamming games. Who said they are lazy? They have been re-educated and primed to use their knowledge appropriately.

Acolyte:

Robbers, kidnappers, hooligans full of all vices the earth has ever known.

Ancestor:

They have encountered the ants for good - they will do well. The nation needs them at this stage of our development. They are being sorted out into appropriate political, social, and economic groups. They will also function in their expected roles. Each one must do what they are practically trained to do. Never again will they roam about with vain theoretical knowledge.

Acolyte:

I am amazed. I am thoroughly amazed. Are you insinuating that they will be the politicians in the new nation? Heeee. The evil bird.

Ancestor:

Definitely. They are capable and they have already started putting things in place under shades of trees. They are organizing. They are organizing well.

Acolyte:

I am just worried about corruption, nepotism, bribery and all sorts of vices.

Ancestor:

Stop looking back. It's a new beginning. It's time to bring the children. Bring the children.

Acolyte:

The houses are not ready, and the schools have not been built.

Ancestor:

They will join their mothers on the fields and get acclimatized. They need to understand the environment and not be afraid of doing things. They need to open their eyes to the entire processes taking place. They must watch the youths and learn from the women. They must roam through the fields and understand the ways of the flora and fauna. They will be fine.

(The shadows guide a group of unseen people from a point designated as the entrance to the ant holes and camps set up by the ants to an exit designated as the entrance to the new nation).

Acolyte:

Interesting.

Ancestor:

It's time to bring in the farmers. They will speedily produce all sorts of crops in the new nation. The ants have taught them to do things naturally without depending on chemicals and the importation of fertilizers.

(The shadows guide a group of unseen people from a point designated as the entrance to the ant holes and camps set up by the ants towards an exit designated as the entrance to the new nation).

Hopefully, we will meet the expected deadline. We are making progress.

Acolyte:

Faster than expected. So why were we lingering in the past?

Ancestor:

Because you all lost the plot. You trusted in others and refused to tune into the inner abilities of the nation. You thought you could never achieve anything without the help of others. So, you became pawns in the hands of your detractors who sold you cheap models of development.

(Ancestor exits while the Shadows appear on stage and begin an inaudible conversation with Acolyte).

The Helpful one:

There is the common will for change. Even in the ant holes, the ants are showing the people great understanding and the people are learning fast. It's not all work and learning. Some of the women who had just completed their training in the ant holes reflected on one of the therapeutic events they enjoyed - the night of a billion fireflies. It was a mixture of fireworks, dance and music, all orchestrated by the ants.

(The night of a billion fireflies is replicated on the stage by the Shadows. There is resounding applause at the end of the performance).

Ancestor:

The framework for effective transportation has been put in place. Bridges, underground sewer systems, good roads, culverts, highways, railways and tram systems - all perfected and deployed. An effective framework has been put in place for the exportation of finished goods. The ports have been dredged at last and expanded to take on trading with nations - far and near. The customs and port officials have been trained and moved to their posts.

(The Shadows appear on the stage in choreographed movement as objects needed for construction are moved across the stage).

Acolyte:

I am afraid - the evil bird.

Ancestor:

What's the problem?

Acolyte:

I am worried about the police force.

Ancestor:

Recruitment is in place in the Camps. Suitable accommodation and allowances are being provided. They are different now.

Acolyte:

Wonderful.

Ancestor:

All systems are in place to generate more funds for the nation and all monies stolen directly or indirectly from the nation are being presently repatriated as we speak. Monies corruptly stolen from public funds are being refunded - including those deposited in obscure places and foreign banks.

Acolyte:

Wonderful.

Ancestor:

How do you all feel about power being democratically transferred to the younger generation who are able to plan the future of the nation?

Acolyte:

Wonderful.

Ancestor:

How do you all feel about Medical centres being developed in all localities with General Medical practitioners posted to specific localities? How do you all feel about the anticipated excellent record on accountability, the end of tribalism and nepotism, cut short by the wholistic form of education introduced by the ants?

Acolyte:

Wonderful.

Ancestor:

What about the fantastic town planning system based on the excellent records of the ants, with their complex and well organised ant hills?

Acolyte:

None of these would work except the educational system and Schools and University curriculum is overhauled drastically.

Ancestor:

That's been put into consideration. The system of education is being tailored to meet the needs of the nation, not to satisfy the whims of the colonial past.

Acolyte:

What about the water and electricity?

Ancestor:

All sorted. They are being privatised and put in the hands of those who are trained to do the job.

Acolyte:

No. You can't do that. I plan to put thousands of generators on loan to many companies and homes in the nation. My water tankers have always been useful to people in the nation.

Ancestor:

Trashed. All trashed. We must begin from the scratch. You would be compensated in a different way, especially with the birth of a new and functional nation. Do your last run and make sure everything is in place before the Independence Day Ceremonies.

Acolyte:

No. We were once independent. Let's keep it that way. Why should those who import foreign foods, sell water in tankers and those who sell electricity generators be punished? This change will affect me drastically; it will certainly affect me.

Ancestor:

It's time to prepare the nation for the Independence ceremonies.

Acolyte:

No. I will not take orders from you. (He screams uncontrollably, showing visible signs of anger and frustration. The evil bird appears and hands him a sword. The wrestling match is fierce, and Ancestor finally wrestled Acolyte to the ground and takes the sword from him).

Ancestor:

You made a great mistake. I can't be killed. I come from a distant past and I work closely with the Creator.

Acolyte:

I am so sorry. Help me.

Ancestor:

You are sorry because you have been overpowered. Now you must share the fate of those who kept the nation perpetually tarnished.

Acolyte:

Is this fair? I served you faithfully. I served the nation.

Ancestor:

Go; join those who thought they served the nation faithfully. Sad - you were considered for the post of the interim President. But you opened your ears to the words of the Evil Bird. The good work will continue. Remember, you were prepared for this.

(Ancestor claps and the Shadows appear, singing a dirge. They lead Acolyte out of the stage in handcuffs).

The Helpful one:

Things are working now. At last. What about the International visitors waiting offshore in ships?

Ancestor:

Let the ants sanitise and indoctrinate them. Go; sort out your nation. My job is done.

The Wailing one:

Please stay permanently with us, so we do not falter, slipping into our old ways.

Ancestor:

You will be fine. I must leave now. (A brief silence envelope the stage as Ancestor exits with the Shadows and the silhouettes of ants forming a guard of honour in the horizon. Celebratory music plays).

The Questioner:

(To the audience) Should the play end this way, or should it end differently?

(The shadows appear, reflecting how the play should end through an improvisation based on the decision of the audience. The play ends with a parade of the Shadows and the silhouettes of the ants).

The End

Conversation

The other version

Cover illustration of the second version of the play by **Hannah Boyd**

BACKGROUND NOTES

The other version of Conversation

This narrative encourages performers to apply meanings freely. It is a diversion from the prescribed form in the first play where most lines or speeches have been written for the characters. The narrative therefore creates the opportunity for the expression of more voices or the variation of perspectives - an experience that is useful in socio-dramatic and community drama contexts, where plays may be conceptualised for community awareness and development purposes. As a playwright, I have always longed to experiment with writing plays that provide the opportunity for the performers to use their creative initiative, rather than have the playwright building the whole narrative picture.

It is important to mention that stylisation may reveal the genius demonstrated in African folktales created and sustained through modification by different authors or performers. Anecdotally, folktales in my part of Africa are usually retold with modifications. One may imagine the dynamism that accompanies the freedom to create and recreate narratives for the benefit of the collective.

The anticipated director, coordinator of the play or performer may include other art forms like singing, dancing, the electronic media to strengthen the meanings that naturally occur in African settings. It is important to mention that the main highlight for dramatisation is the Interventive Enactment which gives the performer the opportunity to address voices and perspectives not related by the Narrator. Finally, this experience gives me the impression that I have found my playwriting voice at last.

Characters

- The Narrator
- Other characters suggested by the Narrator for the Interactive Enactment

Narrator:

Should I say, 'once upon a time,' or should I say, 'It happened suddenly?' Change happened suddenly because folks in my part of Africa were already frustrated by many terrible events around them. Some suggested that the nation should be declared a failed state and others insinuated that the nation should begin from the scratch. Suddenly, there is a massive rumble and the Creator appears and the process of actualising change is put in motion with the Creator empowering the Ants to play a major role. We would revisit this aspect in the narrative.

Interventive Enactment:

Ants parade around the vicinity brandishing different work tools. What sort of rules and regulations would they be announcing to the people to facilitate the lockdown and change process?

Narrator:

You imagine seeing ships heading towards the seashore, and your mind goes to the days of enslavement, when folks from Africa were shipped to strange nations. But the ships that you are seeing presently are not those related to the past; they are related to the present. You are told that the occupants of the ships are from the western world; that they are heading towards our part of Africa because they do not have anywhere else to go - having lost their nations to natural disasters.

Although the children are excited, the adults are not excited about the coming of the international visitors. More people join in asking question and soon, the setting is flooded with more questions as more and more people are interested in asking questions about the second coming of the Europeans. They are described as those who changed our tongues forever, and drove us from the centre, leaving us confused in the periphery. There is a serious debate on what to do. Some folks passionately suggested that they should not be allowed in, others suggested that we must restructure the nation and know how to negotiate sensibly, unlike our forebears before admitting them into the nation.

Interventive Enactment:

Considering the trauma caused by colonialism, why and how might your group enact the negotiation between the people and the international visitors trying to make our part of Africa their new home?

Narrator:

The impression is that the blame is not on the visitors approaching our shores, but on us the collectives. Why? As we all try to find answers to that question, the ships have nearly reached our shores. They are compelled to wait midstream as they watch the body language of the people. In the past, it would have been different.

Interventive Enactment:

If the prospective visitors are given a second chance, what would they do differently? What might the ants teach the people about defending their nation and identity? What might the ants be teaching the visitors about the people?

Narrator:

You begin to wonder why our forebears trusted the colonialists who changed swiftly like the chameleon. They came conquering and looting and snatching all our people knew from their hearts - forcefully. You begin to wonder why your part of Africa is now considered safe when you and others hardly appreciate what you have. It appears that we are the only ones left in the universe. But they cannot come into this state of dysfunction; and the politicians have not been able to fix the mess. You are still wondering how the mess would ever be fixed - then this. You sit there for hours thinking about the visitors and the people; wondering how both parties may integrate. You see images of groups moaning and groaning about everything that has gone wrong. You imagine that worse things may be happening in other developed parts of the world and African has its share. The moaning continues as many complain that nothing has worked in the centre since the colonialists left our shores; Unfortunately, those who dared to speak up were considered as troublemakers by the government. The land continued to degenerate; the nation became a soft spot for neo-colonialist agents who took advantage of soft governments to dictate how the centre should be occupied and milked. The people groaned in pain and suffered. Many of our children were forced to travel across the Sahara Desert to be enslaved again by those whose forebears dragged them into plantations, ripping them of their identities in the guise of introducing civilization.

Interventive Enactment:

How might you react to scenarios where our forebears were told to hate everything that defined them. Were they to blame or did the guns of the colonialist silence them to submission? What might the ants be teaching the people about self-defence?

Narrator:

Then they were all wrapped into a commonwealth where the wealth was not commonly shared. It is disheartening. You would have thought that things would change when those who first colonised us left - making the way for direct and indirect colonisers. How interesting. Such folks are part and parcel of our heritage. How might we react to the notion that we are being internally colonised, or basking in self-colonisation? What about the idea that we are being re-colonised with the script left in the hands of the folks in government? The celebration of independence echoes in your mind - though there are no highlights of obvious economic and political development. Perhaps the politicians were ill-prepared or were certainly not able to read the map of nationhood appropriately. How might you explain what real independence constitutes? What is true Independence? What are the salient signposts for development? You imagine that those who have been victims of the system should have the solutions. Our people would say, he who has the sting, knows how it feels but may not know how it should be treated. You imagine that the opinion of the collective should be sought for one to know what to do. Why did you starve your children and offer nothing to your workers? Why did you frustrate the aged and promise the nation nothing but pain, fear and hunger? Why did you not handle projects like the bridges, dams, railroads and roads that are useful for development? Your long campaign speeches did not save us; yet there were rolls upon rolls of speeches that did not matter much.

Interventive Enactment:

What is true Independence? What could they have done differently to capture the true meaning or essence of liberation? What might the ants be teaching the people about true Independence?

Narrator:

The Creator of the whole universe enters. He is very furious, speaking in a manner that suggests instant change. He instantly introduces a lockdown. The Creator introduces Ancestor who picks Acolyte to work with him to revamp the nation. You wonder how the rules and regulations they are introducing might be coordinated. The main characters introduce the ants, having read a long account of encomiums that designate the ants as peculiar and admirable creatures. The ants are welcomed with much fanfare. Instantly, they go into operation, arresting some and leading many through ant holes into their world for sanitisation and training on the development of the nation.

Interventive Enactment:

Reflect on coups and counter coups. Why were they not effective towards change and development? What might the ants be teaching the people about accepting or culturally modifying democracy?

Narrator:

You reflect on the notion of switching to democracy and things becoming worse. You wonder why prayers don't easily get answered because many have prayed and prayed and died; yet their prayers for good governance were not answered. You imagine that Ancestor should be interrogated on what he gave to the great supernatural power in terms of bribe that opened the door for him to be sent to help clean out the proverbial dirty stable for good. Ancestor is asked this question because nothing has ever been achieved in the nation without bribery and corruption. Ancestor informs the people that he's never taken or given bribes; that he's surprised that many imagine that he would be corrupt.

Interventive Enactment:

What might the ants be teaching the people about transforming the nation?

Narrator:

Acolyte wonders if Ancestor is wired with supernatural technology. Ancestor then states that the power infused in him is the dynamic power of nature. Acolyte retorts, 'I might start taking you seriously if I see myself doing exactly what you are doing.' Acolyte believes that Ancestor is doing what the soldiers could not do - wondering why past governments had corrupt elements. Different groups of people in the nation continue to react excitedly and positively about the news of imminent change. Obviously, they do not complain about being led away by the ants for the much-needed regeneration. You imagine that Ancestor is doing all he can to inform the people on the changes - especially how the nation would be evacuated. You imagine how the ants are busy running about and ordering the people into ant holes - and the nation is abandoned.

Interventive Enactment:

You reflect on a session between Ancestor and the ants as they decide on what to do to change the nation - refining rules.

Narrator:

You imagine how the ants would orchestrate the changes and teach the people new skills which will be useful for change and development. In another conversation you and many others in a drinking spot imagine why the ants are nominated to do this great task. Could it be because they are disciplined and hardworking? You imagine that the ants were specially chosen because they have great skills, wondering how they manage to construct great ant hills that appear on many landscapes. You imagine that the ants are well organised, and that they are different from the soldiers and those voted into government, who take the people for granted.

Interventive Enactment:

The ants are seen in a group as the voice of the Creator is heard giving them instructions on how to continue to work with Ancestor to achieve development, care for the people and make bold changes. Such changes include developing the centre mentality rather than the periphery mentality.

Narrator:

You imagine why the nation is changing rapidly. Folks are complying, listening to the ants and willing to be trained to build. Meanwhile, you imagine how the whole nation is being dismantled into rubbles by Ancestor and the ants and you're wondering how things would be transformed. Then you are given a calm assurance that it would take a moment to dismantle and recreate the whole nation. The conversation is focussed on what Ancestor said, that the change anticipated would be swift and effective. Gradually, the whole nation is being fumigated as more people are seen filing into ant holes to experience the necessary change process. Acolyte kneels, paying homage to Ancestor. Ancestor rebukes him, saying his actions will not be necessary; adding that they have a lot of work to do - that the time frame for the task is one week. One week? You are stunned in your thoughts. You imagine that the nation has been Independent for many years and not developed; so, how would Ancestor change and develop the nation in a week?

Interventive Enactment:

How might the ants be working with academic institutions to develop a unique African identity programme, touching on how the institutions in the nation may adopt changes.

Narrator:

You are forced to interview folks around you about what they think. You begin to imagine how the nation has been dependent for many years, thinking that a sole character may not be able to swing things to positive directions in a few weeks. You reflect on the tribal differences of the people, how illiteracy has been a major problem and how the nation imports everything and anything for sustenance.

Interventive Enactment:

What might the ants be teaching the people about the disadvantages of being importers rather than exporters, knowing that ants are adept importers?

Narrator:

You reflect on how superstitions may have crippled the progress of the nation and the role of the evil bird in the whole situation. The idea of the bird being evil suggests that there would be negative expectations- and you wonder if an evil spell is being cast upon the whole nation. You try to ask a few questions, attempting to know if anyone knows what the presence of an evil bird might signify. You imagine how the ants might be working with the collectives to reverse all the negative and corrupt tendencies held by the politicians in the centre. Everyone is being mobilised; the ants are not prepared to mess around since the task must be done in a week.

Interventive Enactment:

How might the ants sort out the mental health issues in the centre and the periphery, touching on the ridiculous storage of ill-gotten wealth by politicians in odd places and other nations? Also illustrate how such wealth might be used to alleviate the conditions of the poor.

Narrator:

You imagine seeing some ants parading a group of businessmen who appear stubborn - not willing to give up their comfortable houses and amassed wealth. Ancestor orders that they should all be taken into the ant holes for reformation. Acolyte wonders how the ants can tame such corrupt elements. A group of people gathered to interview Ancestor. The interview is followed by a speech about the progress that is being made by the ants. He reports that there is full compliance, and where there have been elements of dissent, the culprits have been swiftly sanitised and appropriately reformed. Whereas Ancestor appears to be angry, and Acolyte confesses that he's afraid of the politicians who can kill, maim and destroy others. You're are surprised to hear that some of the businessmen complained that Ancestor was too strict. The ordinary folks liked his regime and wanted him to continue implementing the new agenda. The people had no choice; they seemed mesmerised completely. Others are amazed about the audacity of the ants as they dealt skilfully with the politicians by arresting and putting them in prison cells. Ancestor clearly explained that the ants are simply fantastic in their roles. Ancestor added that the politicians have completed their work on earth woefully and would be punished for wasting the opportunity they were initially given.

Interventive Enactment:

What might the politicians be saying to each other in their prison cells? What is the usefulness of their lamentations or lack of lamentation? How might the ants be responding to them?

Narrator:

You listen carefully as Acolyte proclaims that all the politicians have been locked up; stating that they are screaming and weeping like children, gnashing their teeth, echoing the Biblical hell. They would have been sitting in their limousines, official cars or private jets criss-crossing the whole earth doing nothing for the people. Now, they are trapped by powers beyond their imagination.

Obviously, they are reaping what they sowed. Acolyte continues by saying that whatever Ancestor is doing is working. He refers to the collectives willingly filing into ant holes to be sanitised and reformed completely. The ants are welcoming them and setting up institutions for them. They are being given books - but the books look different; they are leaves and barks from trees. Acolyte wondered how the ants could be teaching the people to read from leaves and barks of trees - questioning when ants possessed such great knowledge. You pay keen attention when Ancestor says, 'Do not underestimate the power of the Creator of all things. Those were manuscripts we wrote many years ago. You all abandoned them - but the ants preserved them. Even when fragments of them were destroyed by the colonizers in all parts of Africa, some were preserved by the ants in their kingdoms.'

Interventive Enactment:

What might the ants be doing in terms of transforming the mindset of the children and youths who may have imbibed negative ideas from the periphery.

Narrator:

You are inspired to initiate a group discussion after you've been presented with a supernatural drink by Ancestor. Your eyes suddenly pop open and you are enlightened, strengthened and wondering why you have never had such a refreshing drink in your life. It has always been all sorts of sophisticated gins, beers and water imported from foreign nations. You have always been drinking, getting seriously drunk and doing things their own way. Ancestor announces that those who are reformed by the ants in the underground camps should be brought back to the sanitised nation. Acolyte is told to bring in the surveyors and the town planners - having completed their training and empowered to play their part in the nation. Acolyte doubts their loyalty; thinking that they may still ask for bribes thus, continuing with habits associated with underdevelopment. He swears that he knows a few of them who would not undertake any project without asking for bribes. Ancestor assured him that such an era is gone for good because the ants were empowered thousands of years ago to impart the ability to hate bribes. So, Acolyte is assured that the citizens have taken adequate lessons from the ants.

Interventive Enactment:

How might the ants be indoctrinating the people about honesty and good governance in a developing nation?

Narrator:

Acolyte says, 'Look at them; look at them going into action; just like the ants. There seems to be renewed vigour to operate in a new way. This is interesting. We have never seen this before. There has never been such dedication to work and the aptitude to work to instructions.' Ancestor says, the best is yet to come, adding that in the next few years, the whole nation would be transformed, and they would gain what they lost. The engineers are invited into the nation as well as others who would reconstruct roads, generate electricity, build dams for clean water, and build bridges and other infrastructures.

Interventive Enactment:

What might the ants be teaching the people about the importance of the maintenance culture?

Narrator:

Although Acolyte believes that the nation is moving positively towards change, he's surprised that the evil bird is hovering around. Ancestor then says that the evil bird is a good sign. It's there to warn the nation of the need to be focused. Ancestor informs the ants to release the women into the new nation. Acolyte questions what they could have learnt in such a short Space of time, asking if Ancestor really knows them. Ancestor says, 'Bring them in. You do not understand that they are primed to be great learners who can do great things. Unfortunately, they were never given the opportunity to display their knowledge. What could they achieve in an environment corrupted to the core?' Acolyte says, 'You do not know those women. One of them stole the nation deaf and blind. She was sitting in her mansion of gold drinking Krosekko, eating chicken and crying crocodile tears. Ancestor insists that the women should be brought into the new nation, saying, 'Bring them in. They have been programmed to use their great strength to steer the nation towards survival. There is hardly any task they cannot do. They have been better programmed by the ants to do even more. They will fly rockets and go beyond the moon. They will help with the latest machines useful for maximising efforts. You have champions in them.'

Interventive Enactment:

What might the ants have taught the women about assertiveness, empowerment, and development?

Narrator:

Although Acolyte is not convinced about Ancestor's methods, Ancestor reiterates that the era promises positive measures. He added, 'It's time to bring in the youths.' Acolyte is enraged, thinking that Ancestor is gone insane; wondering why such lazy youths would have been transformed in such a short moment. Ancestor cuts in, 'Not this breed of youths. They have not been lazy. They had the ability to undertake all vices with their old and rusty computers. Who said they are lazy? Imagine how the folks in the nation have been re-educated and primed to use their knowledge appropriately.' Acolyte, screams, calling them robbers, kidnappers, hooligans who are full of all vices that the earth has ever known. Ancestor says, 'They have encountered the ants for good -they will do well. The nation needs them at this stage of our development. Go, sort them out into appropriate political, social and economic groups. Get them to begin to function in their expected roles. Each one must do what they are practically trained to do. Never again will they roam about with vain theoretical knowledge.'

Interventive Enactment:

What might the ants be teaching the people about African based education steeped in reformation, touching on decolonisation and the misinformation of the African youth?

Narrator:

Acolyte insinuates that he thoroughly doubts the ability of the youths to form the bedrock of politics in the nation. Ancestor assures him that they are capable and have already started putting things in place under the shades of trees; adding that they are organising well. Acolyte makes us believe that he is worried about corruption, nepotism, bribery and all sorts of vices. He is told to stop looking back since the nation is facing a new beginning. As you are reflecting on the discussion that Acolyte had with

Ancestor, Acolyte is instructed to bring in the children into the new nation, stating that all the houses and schools in the nation have been completed.

Interventive Enactment:

How might the ants develop a new code for meeting the needs of children and empowering the children to play positive roles in the nation?

Narrator:

Ancestor announces that it's time to bring in the farmers, saying, 'They will speedily produce all sorts of crops in the new nation. The ants have taught them to do things naturally without depending on chemicals and the importation of fertilizers.' There is a discussion on the advantages and disadvantages of moving the nation on a fast track. They wonder why the nation lingered so much in the past. Ancestor said, 'Because you all lost the plot. You trusted in others and refused to tune into the inner abilities of the nation. You thought you could never achieve anything without the help of others. So, you became pawns in the hands of your detractors who sold you cheap models of development.'

Interventive Enactment:

What might the ants be teaching the people about cheap development models based on dependency?

Narrator:

The discussion with some folks who just exited underground ant camps coordinated by Acolyte focuses on the idea that the people are being transformed willingly. The people agree that the ants are showing the people great understanding and the people are learning fast. It's not all work and learning. Some of the women who recently exited ant campus reflected on one of the great events they enjoyed which was more therapeutic than any they'd ever witnessed - known as the night of a billion fireflies. It was a mixture of fireworks, dance and music orchestrated by the ants. Ancestor announces that the framework for effective transportation has been put in place. Bridges, underground sewer systems, good roads, culverts, highways, railways and tram systems have all been perfected and deployed. He added that an effective framework has been put in place for the exportation of finished goods to other nations - reiterating that the ports have been dredged and expanded to take on trading with far and near nations. He added that customs and port officials have been trained, motivated and moved to their posts.

Interventive Enactment:

How might the ants be explaining the importance of hard work to the people? The ants teach the people how to take control of their economy, mirroring how they are in control of their own community.

Narrator:

Acolyte informs Ancestor that he is worried about the police force. Ancestor assures him that recruitment is in place; that suitable accommodation and allowances are being provided to motivate them - adding that, 'they are different now.' Ancestor announces that, 'All systems are in place to generate more funds for the nation and all monies stolen directly or indirectly from the nation are being presently repatriated, adding that monies corruptly stolen from public funds are being refunded - including those deposited in obscure places and foreign banks.'

Interventive Enactment:

There is an enactment of the importance of the reparation of monies deposited illegally in foreign banks all around the world by corrupt politicians.

Narrator:

Ancestor said, 'How do you all feel about power being democratically transferred to the younger generation who are able to plan the future of the nation?' As he announces this, the youths are seen taking their place in the nation and assuming roles in the executive, legislative and judicial arm of government. He adds, 'I assured you earlier, they are ready to take over.'

Interventive Enactment:

The youths enact what they were taught by the ants about developing a functional constitution that is relevant for the new nation.

Narrator:

How do you all think about Medical centres being developed in all localities with General Medical practitioners posted to specific localities? Ancestor continued; 'How do you all feel about the anticipated excellent record on accountability, the end of tribalism and nepotism cut short by apt education from the ants? What about the state-of-the-art town planning based on the excellent records of the ants who have complex and well organised systems? Certainly, someone must have something to say about the state of total independence. It's possible, it's possible folks.' Acolyte intoned that 'None of these would work except the educational system and Schools and University curricula are overhauled drastically.' Ancestor assured him that an appropriate system of education has been put in place. Adding that, the system of education is being tailored to meet the needs of the nation, not to satisfy the whims of the colonial past.

Interventive Enactment:

Based on a new Education Curriculum tailored around innate African intelligence, the people enact notions highlighted by the ants touching on education that is focused on the needs of Africans.

Narrator:

Acolyte wants to know what would be done about the provision of water and electricity. Ancestor stated that those areas are being privatised and put in the hands of those who are trained to do the job. But Acolyte is angry, saying, 'No, you can't do that. I had a thousand generators on loan to many companies and homes in the nation. My water tankers have always been useful to people in the nation. Ancestor retorted, 'Trashed. All trashed. We have to begin from the scratch. You would be compensated in a different way, especially with the birth of a new and functional nation. Do your last run and make sure everything is in place before the Independence Day Ceremonies.'

Interventive Enactment:

What might the ants say about Acolyte's attitude considering the recent changes in the nation?

Narrator:

Acolyte is in deep trouble. He stated that the nation was once independent, that it should be kept that way. He added, 'Why should those who import foreign foods, sell water in tanks and those who sell electricity generators be punished? He vehemently stated that the changes will affect him drastically. He then decides not to take orders from Ancestor. Suddenly, the evil bird appears and gives Acolyte a sword. Ancestor wrestles with him and takes the sword from him. Ancestor tells Acolyte that he has been deceived. He informed him that he made a great mistake, adding that he can't be killed because he comes from a distant past and works closely with the Creator. Suddenly, Acolyte is remorseful, saying, 'I am so sorry. Help me.' Ancestor says, 'You are sorry because you have been overpowered. Now you must share the fate of those who kept the nation perpetually tarnished.' Ancestor then says, 'Go; join those who thought they served the nation faithfully. Sad - you were considered for the post of the interim President. But you opened your ears to the words of the Evil Bird. The good work will continue. Remember, you were prepared for this.'

Interventive Enactment:

The question is, should Acolyte be treated like a common criminal, seeing that he served Ancestor faithfully and worked hard to build the nation?

Narrator:

Ancestor speaks to the audience, or a group of people gathered around him, saying, 'should we leave him in the cell or allow him to roam freely in the new nation?' If the decision goes against Acolyte, he would be left in the cell with the corrupt politicians; but if the judgement goes in his favour, he is told the implications of being part of a new nation as indicated by those around trained to serve in the new nation. Somebody asks about the international visitors waiting in ships off the coast. Ancestor's response centres on the people having a conversation on what to do. Ancestor gives his farewell speech and exits in a grand style as the ants and people form a guard of honour, applauding loudly. As soon as the people tearfully bid him farewell, they begin a conversation.

Interventive Enactment:

The enactment is focussed on the pros and cons of integrating the international visitors into the new nation. They discuss how the visitors may be sanitised and trained by the ants to prepare them for the new nation if they all decide to let them in. They take a vote.

The End

THE PLAYWRIGHT'S PROFILE

Isi Agboaye, PhD

Dr Isi Agboaye is a playwright, poet and storyteller who studied at University of Jos, University of Ibadan, and the University of Wolverhampton where he obtained his PhD in Performing Arts. His research is focused on the exploration of postcolonial trauma in his part of Africa, Nigeria, and the diaspora for the purpose of gaining stimulus for playwriting and developing trauma-based plays. His playwriting experiments draw from African folktale contents and postcolonial concepts as underpinning for explaining and understanding the plight of Africans in the continent and the diaspora. He hopes to find a voice for writing and producing plays that highlight decolonization and development. He has been featured in the University of Wolverhampton Artsfest and Black history month, where he organised workshops and performed African Folktales. He has served as visiting lecturer in Creative Writing and Drama at University of Wolverhampton, and Bishop Grosseteste University, Lincoln.

www.ingramcontent.com/pod-product-compliance
Lightning Source LLC
Chambersburg PA
CBHW051004050726
47592CB00007B/2699

* 9 7 8 1 9 0 6 9 6 3 3 3 0 *